CHICAGO PUBLIC LIBRARY

W9-CEN-065

THE SUPER SHOPPER

MEALS IN MINUTES

By Robyn Freedman Spizman
Published by Ivy Books:

GETTING ORGANIZED
KITCHEN 101
FREE AND FABULOUS
SUPERMARKET SECRETS
MEALS IN MINUTES
QUICK TIPS FOR BUSY PEOPLE

Books published by The Ballantine Publishing Group are available at quantity discounts on bulk purchases for premium, educational, fund-raising, and special sales use. For details, please call 1-800-733-3000.

THE SUPER SHOPPER

MEALS IN MINUTES

Robyn Freedman Spizman

IVY BOOKS • NEW YORK

Sale of this book without a front cover may be unauthorized. If this book is coverless, it may have been reported to the publisher as "unsold or destroyed" and neither the author nor the publisher may have received payment for it.

An Ivy Book
Published by The Ballantine Publishing Group
Copyright © 1998 by Robyn Freedman Spizman

All rights reserved under International and Pan-American Copyright Conventions. Published in the United States by The Ballantine Publishing Group, a division of Random House, Inc., New York, and simultaneously in Canada by Random House of Canada Limited, Toronto.

Cover photo © Philip Shone Photography

http://www.randomhouse.com

Library of Congress Catalog Card Number: 97-94255

ISBN 0-8041-1683-0

Manufactured in the United States of America

First Edition: June 1998

10   9   8   7   6   5   4   3   2   1

3ST

R01182 69790

This book is dedicated to you, the reader, for caring enough to choose a healthier way of life for yourself and your family. And to my wonderful parents; family; husband, Willy; and our children, Justin and Ali, for their endless servings of love, support, and understanding.

CHICAGO PUBLIC LIBRARY
BUSINESS / SCIENCE / TECHNOLOGY
400 S. STATE ST.   60605

Contents

Acknowledgments

For starters, a huge helping of thanks goes to my literary agent, Meredith Bernstein, who has served up an enormous amount of support and assistance to me throughout the years. And to my editor, Elisa Wares, Laura Paczosa, and everyone at The Ballantine Publishing Group who contributed the necessary ingredients to make this book possible. A special thanks also goes to the talented and enthusiastic Mary Ann Lukas of Harry's Farmers Market for all her valuable help in the preparation and creation of this book. No kitchen should be without Mary Ann's bright advice and low-fat ideas! And finally, thanks to Melanie Houser for her tremendous assistance and guidance in the nutritional analysis of each recipe.

THE SUPER SHOPPER

MEALS IN MINUTES

Introduction

Perhaps you're like me. You enjoy eating but prefer to spend less time in the kitchen cooking. Or you enjoy eating but would prefer to eat foods that are lower in fat. Well, help has arrived! This book presents not only simple-to-make meals but also a variety of recipes that are lower in fat for creative meal planning.

You might have also purchased this book because you're trying to lose weight. There are no magic formulas for doing so, but there *are* creative alternatives and super solutions for making cooking with less fat fun.

The real secret to losing weight and maintaining a healthy lifestyle is to understand exactly what you are eating. Just because something's low in fat doesn't mean it's low in calories. So be an educated eater, an informed consumer, and take charge of your eating habits. Observe the portions you are consuming and read labels carefully.

Consider the nutritional analysis for the recipes you select, and discover healthier ways to prepare your favorite recipes. You'll be surprised how easy it is to lower the fat and calories in the foods you already love to make. You will not only enjoy the food more, but you'll make educated choices for a lifetime of healthy eating.

Note: This is not meant to be a diet book. Some of the ingredients may not be appropriate for those on restricted diets. Also, remember that serving sizes may vary, and nutritional information should be based according to actual portion size.

1

Appetizers

Salmon Roulade Wrap-Up

3/4 cup fat-free cream cheese, softened
4 (10-inch) fat-free flour tortillas
Salt and freshly ground pepper
3/4 pound thinly sliced smoked salmon
1 bunch chives

Spread cream cheese evenly over one side of each tortilla. Season to taste with salt and pepper. Lay smoked salmon slices in one layer over the cream cheese and top with chives. Roll the tortillas as tightly as possible. Slice into 1-inch pieces and arrange on a serving platter.
Yield: 3 dozen

Nutritional Facts per Serving:
1 Piece (28g): 40 Calories, 0 Fat Calories, 0g Fat, 0g Saturated Fat, 5mg Cholesterol, 370mg Sodium, 4g Carbohydrate, 0g Dietary Fiber, 0g Sugars, 4g Protein, 4% (DV) Vitamin A, 0% (DV) Vitamin C, 4% (DV) Calcium, 2% (DV) Iron

Santa Fe Black Bean
Tortilla Pinwheels

1 (8-ounce) container fat-free cream cheese
1 cup fat-free sour cream
1 cup shredded reduced-fat Monterey Jack cheese
$1/4$ cup chopped red onion
1 teaspoon fresh cilantro, minced (optional)
$1/2$ teaspoon seasoned salt
$1/8$ teaspoon garlic powder
1 (15-ounce) can black beans, drained
5 (10-inch) fat-free flour tortillas
Prepared salsa

Beat the cream cheese and sour cream in a medium bowl until well blended. Stir in Monterey Jack cheese, onion, cilantro (if using), salt, and garlic powder. Cover and refrigerate for 15 minutes. Place beans in a food processor; process until smooth. Spread a thin layer of the beans over each tortilla. Follow with a thin layer of the cream cheese mixture. Roll tortillas tightly. Wrap in plastic and refrigerate until chilled. Cut tortillas into $3/4$-inch slices and arrange on a platter. Serve with salsa.

Yield: 15 pinwheels

Nutritional Facts per Serving:

1 Pinwheel (93g): 90 Calories, 10 Fat Calories, 1g Fat, 1g Saturated Fat, 5mg Cholesterol, 520mg Sodium, 4g Carbohydrate, 2g Dietary Fiber, 2g Sugars, 6g Protein, 8% (DV) Vitamin A, 0% (DV) Vitamin C, 10% (DV) Calcium, 4% (DV) Iron

Super Spinach Dip

2 cups fat-free plain yogurt
1 (10-ounce) package frozen chopped spinach, thawed and squeezed
  dry
1/3 cup finely chopped onion (preferably Vidalia)
2 tablespoons fat-free mayonnaise
1 (1.4-ounce) package instant vegetable soup mix

In a medium bowl combine yogurt, spinach, onion, mayonnaise, and
vegetable soup mix; mix well. Serve with assorted raw vegetables for
dipping.
Yield: about 3 cups

Nutritional Facts per Serving:

2 Tablespoons (28g): 20 Calories, 0 Fat Calories, 0g Fat, 0g Saturated
Fat, 0mg Cholesterol, 140mg Sodium, 3g Carbohydrate, <1g Dietary
Fiber, 2g Sugars, 2g Protein, 20% (DV) Vitamin A, 6% (DV) Vitamin C,
6% (DV) Calcium, 2% (DV) Iron

Crab Horseradish Dip

$1/2$ cup undiluted evaporated skim milk
1 (8-ounce) package fat-free cream cheese, softened
$3/4$ cup imitation crabmeat, shredded
2 tablespoons minced green onion
2 tablespoons finely chopped red bell pepper
2 teaspoons prepared horseradish
$1/4$ teaspoon garlic salt

In a small mixing bowl, beat evaporated skim milk and cream cheese. Stir in crabmeat, onion, red pepper, horseradish, and garlic salt. Cover and refrigerate. Serve with assorted raw vegetables.
Yield: about 2 cups

Nutritional Facts per Serving:

2 Tablespoons (28g): 25 Calories, 0 Fat Calories, 0g Fat, 0g Saturated Fat, 5mg Cholesterol, 105mg Sodium, 2g Carbohydrate, 0g Dietary Fiber, 1g Sugars, 3g Protein, 6% (DV) Vitamin A, 2% (DV) Vitamin C, 6% (DV) Calcium, 0% (DV) Iron

Baked Tortilla Chips

1 package fat-free flour (or corn) tortillas

Preheat oven to 350 degrees F. Stack fat-free flour tortillas and cut into wedges. Place tortilla wedges in a single layer on an ungreased baking sheet. Bake for approximately 10 minutes, or until crisp. Serve with your favorite fat-free black bean dip or salsa.

Nutritional Facts per Serving:

1/2 tortilla (30g): 100 Calories, 20 Fat Calories, 2.5g Fat, 0g Saturated Fat, 0mg Cholesterol, 150mg Sodium, 18g Carbohydrate, <1g Dietary Fiber, 0g Sugars, 3g Protein, 0% (DV) Vitamin A, 0% (DV) Vitamin C, 4% (DV) Calcium, 6% (DV) Iron

Spicy Quesadillas with Jalapeño Cheese

1 teaspoon olive oil
2 onions, sliced thin
1 red pepper, sliced thin
1 green pepper, sliced thin
1 yellow pepper, sliced thin
2 tablespoons minced jalapeños
2 cloves garlic, minced
Salt and freshly ground pepper
6 fat-free flour tortillas
1 (8-ounce) jar salsa
12 ounces fat-free Cheddar, grated
Fat-free sour cream (optional)

In a skillet, heat olive oil. Sauté onions and peppers until soft. Add garlic. Cook for 1 minute. Remove from heat. Season to taste with salt and pepper. Lay out tortillas. Spread salsa on half of each tortilla; spread the onion-pepper mixture and cheese over the salsa. Fold once, creating a half-moon shape. In a hot cast-iron skillet, brown tortilla half moons on both sides, approximately 1 to 2 minutes per side. Remove and cut each tortilla into four wedges. Serve with additional salsa and fat-free sour cream, if desired.
Yield: 6 servings of 4 wedges each

Nutritional Facts per Serving:
260 Calories, 10 Fat Calories, 1g Fat, 0g Saturated Fat, 5mg Cholesterol,

1390mg Sodium, 38g Carbohydrate, 2g Dietary Fiber, 9g Sugars, 22g Protein, 30% (DV) Vitamin A, 100% (DV) Vitamin C, 90% (DV) Calcium, 8% (DV) Iron

2

Salads

Light Coleslaw

$^1/_3$ cup fat-free Miracle Whip
$^1/_4$ cup cider vinegar
1 tablespoon creamy mustard
Salt and freshly ground pepper
1 (16-ounce) package fresh coleslaw mix

In a medium-size bowl, combine Miracle Whip, vinegar, mustard, and salt and pepper to taste. Toss with coleslaw mix and serve.
Yield: 4 servings

Nutritional Facts per Serving:
60 Calories, 10 Fat Calories, 1g Fat, 0g Saturated Fat, 0mg Cholesterol, 710mg Sodium, 11g Carbohydrate, 3g Dietary Fiber, 7g Sugars, 2g Protein, 160% (DV) Vitamin A, 50% (DV) Vitamin C, 4% (DV) Calcium, 4% (DV) Iron

Cool Cucumber Salad

1 cup fat-free plain yogurt
2 tablespoons thinly sliced scallions
$1/2$ teaspoon vegetable oil
1 tablespoon fresh lemon or lime juice
1 tablespoon minced fresh parsley
1 teaspoon honey or sugar
Salt, freshly ground pepper, and paprika
$1^1/2$ cups thinly sliced cucumber
Lettuce leaves

In a medium-size bowl, combine yogurt, scallions, oil, lemon juice, and parsley. Stir in honey; season to taste with salt, pepper, and paprika. Add cucumber and toss gently. Serve on lettuce leaves.

Note: Long, slender English or European cucumbers are a boon to busy cooks. They are seedless and unwaxed, so seeding and peeling are not necessary. Simply rinse off cucumbers and slice in food processor for an almost instant salad.

Yield: 4 servings

Nutritional Facts per Serving:

70 Calories, 20 Fat Calories, 2g Fat, 0g Saturated Fat, 0mg Cholesterol, 320mg Sodium, 9g Carbohydrate, <1g Dietary Fiber, 8g Sugars, 4g Protein, 6% (DV) Vitamin A, 10% (DV) Vitamin C, 15% (DV) Calcium, 2% (DV) Iron

Grilled Honey-Mustard Chicken over Mixed Greens

The sauce:
3 tablespoons honey
3 tablespoons oriental spicy-style mustard
1/2 teaspoon grated lemon peel
1 teaspoon fresh lemon juice
1 teaspoon reduced-sodium soy sauce
1/2 teaspoon garlic salt

The salad:
4 boneless, skinless chicken breast halves
1/4 teaspoon salt
1/4 teaspoon freshly ground pepper
1 (10-ounce) package mixed salad greens
1/2 cup fat-free honey-Dijon salad dressing

Spray grill with nonstick cooking spray and heat. In small bowl, combine honey, mustard, lemon peel, lemon juice, soy sauce, and garlic salt; blend well. Set aside. Sprinkle both sides of chicken with salt and pepper. Place chicken on grill over medium heat. Brush chicken with sauce; cook 4 to 6 minutes. Turn chicken; brush generously with remaining sauce. Cook an additional 4 to 6 minutes or until chicken is tender and juices run clear. In a large bowl, combine salad greens and dressing; toss to mix. To serve, cut chicken into strips or bite-size pieces. Add chicken to salad; toss, if desired.
Yield: 4 servings

Nutritional Facts per Serving:

240 Calories, 30 Fat Calories, 3g Fat, 1g Saturated Fat, 70mg Cholesterol, 960mg Sodium, 24g Carbohydrate, 3g Dietary Fiber, 20g Sugars, 27g Protein, 40% (DV) Vitamin A, 20% (DV) Vitamin C, 6% (DV) Calcium, 10% (DV) Iron

Chicken Caesar Salad

8 cups lightly packed torn romaine lettuce
1 cup cooked boneless, skinless chicken breast, cut up
3 tablespoons grated fresh Parmesan cheese
3/4 cup prepared fat-free Caesar salad dressing
1 cup prepared croutons

Place romaine and chicken in a large salad bowl. Sprinkle with Parmesan cheese. Toss with salad dressing and top with croutons. Serve immediately.
Yield: 4 servings

Nutritional Facts per Serving:

180 Calories, 45 Fat Calories, 5g Fat, 2g Saturated Fat, 35mg Cholesterol, 780mg Sodium, 15g Carbohydrate, 2g Dietary Fiber, 4g Sugars, 17g Protein, 60% (DV) Vitamin A, 45% (DV) Vitamin C, 10% (DV) Calcium, 10% (DV) Iron

Pasta-Cheese-and-Vegetable Salad

2 cups rotini and/or penne or other short pasta
2 cups broccoli florets
1 1/2 cups reduced-fat Cheddar, cubed small
10 cherry tomatoes, quartered
1 green and/or red sweet bell pepper, chopped
2 green onions, thinly sliced
1 tablespoon olive oil
2 tablespoons red wine vinegar
2 tablespoons fresh basil, snipped (or 1/2 teaspoon dried basil, crushed)
1/4 teaspoon salt
1/4 teaspoon freshly ground pepper

Cook pasta according to package directions until al dente (firm to the bite), adding broccoli florets for the last 5 minutes of cooking. Drain, rinse, and drain again. Combine pasta-broccoli mixture, cheese, tomatoes, bell pepper, and onions in a large bowl. Combine oil, vinegar, basil, salt, and pepper in a screw-top jar; shake well to mix. Pour over pasta mixture. Cover and refrigerate 2 hours or until ready to serve.
Yield: 6 servings

Nutritional Facts per Serving:
200 Calories, 45 Fat Calories, 5g Fat, 1.5g Saturated Fat, 5mg Cholesterol, 380mg Sodium, 27g Carbohydrate, 3g Dietary Fiber, 3g Sugars, 12g Protein, 15% (DV) Vitamin A, 60% (DV) Vitamin C, 20% (DV) Calcium, 10% (DV) Iron

Garden Salad with Fresh Grapes

1 teaspoon extra-virgin olive oil
1 tablespoon raspberry vinegar
1 tablespoon fresh lemon juice
2 tablespoons water
1 shallot, chopped
2 teaspoons Dijon mustard
1/4 teaspoon dried tarragon, crushed
Freshly ground pepper
4 cups torn mixed salad greens
1 cup seedless grapes (red or green)

Whisk together oil, vinegar, lemon juice, water, shallot, mustard, tarragon, and pepper in a small bowl until well blended; set aside. In a large bowl combine mixed greens and grapes. Toss with dressing. Serve at once.

Yield: 4 servings

Nutritional Facts per Serving:

60 Calories, 15 Fat Calories, 2g Fat, 0g Saturated Fat, 0mg Cholesterol, 80mg Sodium, 11g Carbohydrate, 1g Dietary Fiber, 9g Sugars, 1g Protein, 30% (DV) Vitamin A, 25% (DV) Vitamin C, 4% (DV) Calcium, 6% (DV) Iron

Festive Fruit Salad with Strawberry-Yogurt Dressing

The salad:
1 fresh pineapple
2 oranges, peeled and sliced
2 bananas, peeled and sliced
1 cup fresh strawberries, washed, hulled, and sliced
1 cup seedless grapes

The dressing:
6 fresh strawberries, washed, hulled, and halved
1 banana, peeled and sliced
1 cup fat-free vanilla yogurt
1 tablespoon brown sugar (packed) or honey

Cut pineapple in half lengthwise through crown. Cut pineapple from shells, leaving shells intact. Cut pineapple into chunks. In a large bowl combine pineapple, oranges, bananas, strawberries, and grapes. Toss together. Spoon into pineapple shells and chill. For the dressing, place strawberries, banana, yogurt, and brown sugar in a food processor or blender and process until smooth. Serve over fresh fruit.
Yield: 6 servings

Nutritional Facts per Serving:
170 Calories, 10 Fat Calories, 1g Fat, 0g Saturated Fat, 30mg Cholesterol, 30mg Sodium, 42g Carbohydrate, 3g Dietary Fiber, 36g Sugars, 4g Protein, 4% (DV) Vitamin A, 120% (DV) Vitamin C, 10% (DV) Calcium, 4% (DV) Iron

Southwestern Salsa Chicken Salad

1 garlic clove, minced
$1/2$ pound boneless, skinless chicken breasts
1 (16-ounce) can California cling peaches in natural juice
$1/2$ teaspoon chili powder
$1/4$ teaspoon ground cumin
$3/4$ teaspoon seasoned salt
1 head iceberg lettuce, rinsed and crisped in refrigerator for
   30 minutes
1 (10$1/2$-ounce) box frozen corn, cooked, drained, and cooled
1 cup cherry tomatoes, halved
$1/2$ cup sliced green onion
$1/2$ cup minced cilantro
1 (4-ounce) can diced green chilies, drained

Bring 2 cups water to a boil; add garlic. Add chicken breasts. Simmer 10 to 15 minutes until cooked through. Drain, cool, and shred chicken breasts. Drain peach slices, reserving $1/4$ cup liquid. Cut peaches in half and set aside. Mix reserved peach juice with chili powder, cumin, and seasoned salt for dressing. Set aside. Cut lettuce into chunks and place in a bowl with shredded chicken, peach slices, corn, tomatoes, onion, cilantro, and chilies. Drizzle with salad dressing and toss well just before serving.
Yield: 4 servings

Nutritional Facts per Serving:
190 Calories, 15 Fat Calories, 1.5g Fat, 0g Saturated Fat, 30mg

Cholesterol, 350mg Sodium, 33g Carbohydrate, 5g Dietary Fiber, 16g Sugars, 16g Protein, 25% (DV) Vitamin A, 50% (DV) Vitamin C, 4% (DV) Calcium, 10% (DV) Iron

Spring Fruit and Garden Greens Salad

The dressing:
4 tablespoons fat-free plain yogurt
2 teaspoons sugar
2 teaspoons fresh lemon juice

The salad:
3 cups mixed salad greens
2 oranges, peeled and cubed
2 apples, cored and cubed
2 teaspoons chopped walnuts

Combine yogurt, sugar, and lemon juice in a small bowl; blend well and chill. Place greens, oranges, and apples in salad bowl; toss to combine. Pour dressing over salad; sprinkle with walnuts.
Yield: 4 servings

Nutritional Facts per Serving:
100 Calories, 10 Fat Calories, 1g Fat, 0g Saturated Fat, 0mg Cholesterol, 20 mg Sodium, 22g Carbohydrate, 3g Dietary Fiber, 18g Sugars, 2g Protein, 25% (DV) Vitamin A, 80% (DV) Vitamin C, 8% (DV) Calcium, 4% (DV) Iron

Italian Turkey Salad

3 cups finely shredded romaine lettuce
1/2 cup fat-free Italian salad dressing
2 cups (12 ounces) thin strips cooked turkey breast
2 cups chopped fresh tomatoes
1 tablespoon minced fresh basil

Place romaine in a large bowl. Toss with salad dressing. Arrange lettuce on 4 serving plates, dividing evenly. Place tomatoes and basil on each plate alongside turkey strips and serve.
Yield: 4 servings

Nutritional Facts per Serving:

150 Calories, 15 Fat Calories, 1.5g Fat, 0g Saturated Fat, 75mg Cholesterol, 340mg Sodium, 7g Carbohydrate, 1g Dietary Fiber, 5g Sugars, 27g Protein, 35% (DV) Vitamin A, 45% (DV) Vitamin C, 4% (DV) Calcium, 10% (DV) Iron

Asian Chicken and Rice Salad

3 cups cooked rice, cooled
1 cup cooked chicken breast pieces
1 cup sliced celery
1 can sliced water chestnuts, drained
1 cup fresh bean sprouts
1/2 cup sliced fresh mushrooms
1/4 cup minced green onions
1/4 cup diced red bell pepper
3 tablespoons fresh lemon juice
2 tablespoons reduced-sodium soy sauce
11/2 tablespoons sesame oil
2 teaspoons grated fresh ginger
1/4 teaspoon ground white pepper
12 to 14 lettuce leaves

Combine rice, chicken, celery, water chestnuts, bean sprouts, mushrooms, onions, and red pepper in a large bowl. Put lemon juice, soy
sauce, oil, ginger, and white pepper in a jar with lid; shake well until
blended. Pour over rice mixture and toss. Serve on lettuce leaves.
Yield: 6 servings

Nutritional Facts per Serving:
180 Calories, 50 Fat Calories, 6g Fat, 1g Saturated Fat, 20mg Cholesterol, 490mg Sodium, 22g Carbohydrate, 3g Dietary Fiber, 3g Sugars,
11g Protein, 8% (DV) Vitamin A, 30% (DV) Vitamin C, 4% (DV) Calcium, 10% (DV) Iron

Tangy Turkey Pasta Salad

2 cups (8 ounces) turkey breast cut into julienne strips
2 cups farfalle (bow tie) or shell pasta, cooked and drained
1 (8-ounce) bag assorted frozen vegetables, thawed
6 cherry tomatoes, halved
³/₄ cup fat-free Italian or fat-free vinaigrette dressing
4 cups mixed greens, washed and drained, or prepacked

Combine turkey, pasta, vegetables, tomatoes, and salad dressing in a large bowl; toss well. Cover and refrigerate 10 minutes before serving to allow flavors to blend. Serve on top of greens.
Yield: 6 servings

Nutritional Facts per Serving:

160 Calories, 10 Fat Calories, 1g Fat, 0g Saturated Fat, 35mg Cholesterol, 340mg Sodium, 22g Carbohydrate, 3g Dietary Fiber, 3g Sugars, 16g Protein, 60% (DV) Vitamin A, 20% (DV) Vitamin C, 4% (DV) Calcium, 10% (DV) Iron

Surefire Shrimp and Pasta Salad

8 ounces medium pasta shells
2 cups medium cooked shrimp, shelled and deveined
2 cups fresh tomatoes, chopped
2 cups torn spinach
1 cup fresh cauliflower florets
$1/2$ cup sliced radishes
$1/4$ cup sliced green onion
1 tablespoon vegetable oil
2 tablespoons fresh lemon juice
1 tablespoon Dijon mustard
$1/4$ teaspoon dried thyme leaves, crushed
$1/4$ teaspoon lemon pepper seasoning

Cook pasta according to package directions and drain. In a large bowl, combine pasta, shrimp, tomatoes, spinach, cauliflower, radishes, and onion. In a small bowl, whisk together oil, lemon juice, mustard, thyme, and seasoning; drizzle over shrimp mixture and toss to coat. Cover; refrigerate. Toss gently before serving.
Yield: 10 servings

Nutritional Facts per Serving:
150 Calories, 20 Fat Calories, 2.5g Fat, 0g Saturated Fat, 55mg Cholesterol, 125mg Sodium, 22g Carbohydrate, 2g Dietary Fiber, 3g Sugars, 10g Protein, 20% (DV) Vitamin A, 30% (DV) Vitamin C, 4% (DV) Calcium, 15% (DV) Iron

Chicken Taco Salad

1 pound boneless, skinless chicken breast, sliced
1 tablespoon vegetable oil
1 tablespoon chili powder
1 (16-ounce) package salad greens
1 (8-ounce) jar salsa
1 (8-ounce) bottle fat-free ranch dressing
1 cup shredded fat-free Cheddar cheese
1/2 cup baked tortilla chips, crushed (optional)

Cook chicken in oil and chili powder in a large nonstick skillet on medium-high for 8 minutes or until chicken is cooked through. Toss chicken mixture, greens, salsa, dressing, and cheese in a large bowl. Top with crushed tortilla chips, if desired.

Yield: 6 servings

Nutritional Facts per Serving:

210 Calories, 40 Fat Calories, 4.5g Fat, 1g Saturated Fat, 45mg Cholesterol, 870mg Sodium, 18g Carbohydrate, 2g Dietary Fiber, 10g Sugars, 23g Protein, 60% (DV) Vitamin A, 25% (DV) Vitamin C, 35% (DV) Calcium, 10% (DV) Iron

Spill-the-Beans Salsa Salad

1 (15-ounce) can red beans, rinsed and drained
1/4 cup minced green onions
1 large tomato, seeded and chopped
1 serrano pepper, seeded and chopped
1 tablespoon chopped fresh cilantro
1 tablespoon fresh lime juice
1/4 teaspoon salt
1/4 teaspoon freshly ground pepper

In a medium bowl, combine all ingredients; mix well. Cover and refrigerate to allow flavors to blend. Serve with baked tortilla chips.
Yield: 5 servings

Nutritional Facts per Serving:

80 Calories, 0 Fat Calories, 0g Fat, 0g Saturated Fat, 0mg Cholesterol, 400mg Sodium, 15g Carbohydrate, 6g Dietary Fiber, 2g Sugars, 5g Protein, 2% (DV) Vitamin A, 20% (DV) Vitamin C, 2% (DV) Calcium, 6% (DV) Iron

3

Poultry

Turkey Taco Burgers

1 pound ground turkey breast
1/4 cup salsa
4 pita breads
1/4 cup fat-free sour cream
1 cup shredded lettuce
1/2 cup diced tomatoes
1/2 cup shredded fat-free Cheddar

Combine turkey and salsa. Shape into 4 burgers. Broil burgers 4 inches from heat until well-done (approximately 10 to 12 minutes), turning once. To assemble sandwiches, slit top of each pita to form a pocket. Place burgers in pita pockets. Top with sour cream, lettuce, tomatoes, and cheese.
Yield: 4 servings

Nutritional Facts per Serving:

310 Calories, 20 Fat Calories, 2.5g Fat, .5g Saturated Fat, 80mg Cholesterol, 640mg Sodium, 31g Carbohydrate, 4g Dietary Fiber, 4g Sugars, 41g Protein, 15% (DV) Vitamin A, 8% (DV) Vitamin C, 45% (DV) Calcium, 15% (DV) Iron

Mexican Chicken Potatoes

4 medium baking potatoes
1 tablespoon butter
$^1/_2$ cup sliced green onions
2 cups shredded or diced cooked chicken breast
1 cup fat-free sour cream
Salsa (optional)

Pierce potatoes with fork; place on paper towel in microwave. Microwave on High until tender (15 to 18 minutes), turning once. Meanwhile, in an 8-inch skillet, melt butter; stir in green onions. Cook over medium-high heat, stirring occasionally, for 1 minute. Add chicken and sour cream. Continue cooking, stirring occasionally, until heated through (1 to 2 minutes). Split hot potatoes; top each with about $^1/_2$ cup of the chicken mixture. Garnish with salsa, if desired.
Yield: 4 servings

Nutritional Facts per Serving:

350 Calories, 60 Fat Calories, 6g Fat, 2.5g Saturated Fat, 65mg Cholesterol, 140mg Sodium, 42g Carbohydrate, 3g Dietary Fiber, 6g Sugars, 28g Protein, 10% (DV) Vitamin A, 30% (DV) Vitamin C, 10% (DV) Calcium, 15% (DV) Iron

Chicken and Oriental Noodles

1 tablespoon sesame oil
1 pound boneless, skinless chicken breasts, cut into 2 × 1/2-inch strips
1 (16-ounce) package pre-cut fresh (or frozen) stir-fry vegetables
1/2 tablespoon minced garlic
2 scallions, minced
1 package low-fat oriental flavor ramen noodle soup

In large skillet heat oil; add chicken. Cook over medium-high heat, stirring occasionally, until chicken is no longer pink (5 to 6 minutes). Add vegetables, garlic, scallions, and seasoning packet from soup. Continue cooking, stirring occasionally, until vegetables are crisp-tender (5 to 6 minutes). Meanwhile, cook ramen noodles according to package directions; drain. Stir noodles into chicken-vegetable mixture. Cook 1 minute. Serve immediately.

Note: If you are using frozen vegetables, thaw according to package directions.

Yield: 4 servings

Nutritional Facts per Serving:

370 Calories, 70 Fat Calories, 7g Fat, 1.5g Saturated Fat, 65mg Cholesterol, 920mg Sodium, 48g Carbohydrate, 7g Dietary Fiber, 6g Sugars, 31g Protein, 100% (DV) Vitamin A, 6% (DV) Vitamin C, 4% (DV) Calcium, 20% (DV) Iron

Balsamic Vinaigrette Grilled Chicken and Summer Vegetables

$1/4$ cup balsamic vinegar

2 teaspoons olive oil

$1^1/2$ teaspoons minced garlic

1 tablespoon Dijon mustard

$1/2$ teaspoon dried rosemary, crushed

$1/4$ teaspoon coarsely ground black pepper

1 pound boneless, skinless chicken breasts

2 red onions, cut into 6 wedges

1 eggplant, cut into 1-inch rounds

1 yellow pepper, cut into 2-inch strips

1 sweet red pepper, cut into 2-inch strips

8 ounces capellini (angel hair) pasta, cooked and drained

In a 9 × 13-inch glass baking dish, combine vinegar, oil, garlic, mustard, rosemary, and black pepper. Add chicken, turning to coat with marinade. Cover and refrigerate for 10 minutes. Add onions, eggplant, and peppers to mixture. Arrange chicken and vegetables on a hot grill, reserving marinade. Cook, turning chicken and vegetables occasionally and brushing them with reserved marinade, until chicken is cooked through and vegetables are tender, about 8 to 10 minutes. Serve over pasta.

Yield: 6 servings

Nutritional Facts per Serving:

200 Calories, 35 Fat Calories, 4g Fat, 1g Saturated Fat, 40mg Cholesterol,

105mg Sodium, 23g Carbohydrate, 3g Dietary Fiber, 9g Sugars, 19g Protein, 10% (DV) Vitamin A, 80% (DV) Vitamin C, 4% (DV) Calcium, 10% (DV) Iron

Garlic Salsa Chicken

4 boneless, skinless chicken breast halves
1 tablespoon vegetable oil
1 garlic clove, minced
1 1/2 cups salsa
Fat-free sour cream
1 lemon, cut into wedges

In a skillet, brown chicken in oil over medium-high heat, 4 to 5 minutes
per side. Reduce heat and pour garlic and salsa over chicken; cook
2 minutes. Serve with a dollop of sour cream and a wedge of lemon.
Yield: 4 servings

Nutritional Facts per Serving:

310 Calories, 60 Fat Calories, 7g Fat, 1.5g Saturated Fat, 75mg Cholesterol, 880mg Sodium, 27g Carbohydrate, <1g Dietary Fiber, 9g Sugars, 34g Protein, 25% (DV) Vitamin A, 50% (DV) Vitamin C, 20% (DV)
Calcium, 10% (DV) Iron

Salsa Chicken Sauté

3 boneless, skinless chicken breast halves, cut into strips
1 tablespoon vegetable oil
1 onion, cut into thin strips
1 medium bell pepper, cut into strips
1¹/₂ cups salsa

In skillet, sauté chicken in oil over medium-high heat for 3 minutes. Add onion and pepper strips; cook 3 to 4 minutes, until tender and crisp. Reduce heat; add salsa and simmer for 2 minutes.
Yield: 4 servings

Nutritional Facts per Serving:

190 Calories, 50 Fat Calories, 6g Fat, 1g Saturated Fat, 55mg Cholesterol, 800mg Sodium, 11g Carbohydrate, 2g Dietary Fiber, 6g Sugars, 22g Protein, 15% (DV) Vitamin A, 35% (DV) Vitamin C, 10% (DV) Calcium, 8% (DV) Iron

Chicken Pasta Primavera

6 ounces (2 cups) farfalle (bow tie) pasta
10 ounces (2 cups) fresh baby-cut carrots
$1/2$ pound fresh asparagus, trimmed, cut into 1-inch pieces
$1/2$ cup fresh broccoli florets
1 cup skim milk
2 tablespoons all-purpose flour
$11/2$ teaspoons reduced-sodium chicken broth or instant bouillon
Freshly ground pepper
4 boneless, skinless chicken breast halves, cut into bite-size pieces
$1/3$ cup finely shredded fresh Parmesan cheese
Chopped fresh chives (optional)

Cook pasta and carrots in boiling water for 8 to 10 minutes or until de-sired doneness, adding asparagus and broccoli during the last minute of cooking time. Meanwhile, in small bowl, blend milk, flour, broth, and pepper. Set aside. Spray large nonstick skillet with cooking spray. Heat over medium-high flame until water evaporates when splashed onto pan. Add chicken; cook and stir 4 to 6 minutes or until chicken is lightly browned and cooked through. Add milk mixture to skillet; cook and stir 2 to 3 minutes, or until bubbly and thickened. Stir in Parmesan cheese; cook over medium-low heat until cheese is melted, stirring constantly. Drain pasta and vegetables. Add to chicken mixture; toss gently to combine. Sprinkle with chopped fresh chives before serving, if desired.
Yield: 6 servings

Nutritional Facts per Serving:

270 Calories, 40 Fat Calories, 4.5g Fat, 2g Saturated Fat, 55mg Cholesterol, 310mg Sodium, 29g Carbohydrate, 3g Dietary Fiber, 6g Sugars, 27g Protein, 220% (DV) Vitamin A, 15% (DV) Vitamin C, 15% (DV) Calcium, 15% (DV) Iron

Marinated Chicken Kabobs

4 boneless, skinless chicken breasts
2 small zucchini, cut into $1/2$-inch slices
1 red bell pepper, cut into 1-inch squares
$1/4$ cup fat-free Italian dressing

Lightly flatten chicken breasts. Cut into cubes. Place chicken in a bowl with zucchini and bell pepper. Toss with dressing. Cover and refrigerate for 10 minutes. Drain marinade into a small saucepan and boil. Alternately thread chicken and vegetables onto skewers; brush with marinade. Broil 3 to 5 inches from heat source until chicken is done (about 8 to 10 minutes), turning and brushing with marinade after 5 minutes.
Yield: 4 servings

Nutritional Facts per Serving:
150 Calories, 25 Fat Calories, 3g Fat, 1g Saturated Fat, 70mg Cholesterol, 190mg Sodium, 3g Carbohydrate, <1g Dietary Fiber, 2g Sugars, 26g Protein, 15% (DV) Vitamin A, 50% (DV) Vitamin C, 2% (DV) Calcium, 6% (DV) Iron

Chicken Fajitas

$^1/_2$ tablespoon vegetable oil
1 large green bell pepper, thinly sliced
1 large red bell pepper, thinly sliced
1 large red onion, thinly sliced
1 garlic clove, minced
4 boneless, skinless chicken breasts, cut into $^1/_2$-inch strips
$^1/_2$ teaspoon dried oregano, crushed
2 tablespoons water
Salt and freshly ground black pepper
12 fat-free flour tortillas

Heat oil in a large skillet over medium flame. Add peppers, onion, and garlic. Cook 3 to 4 minutes or until crisp-tender, stirring occasionally. Remove vegetables with slotted spoon; set aside. Add chicken and oregano to skillet. Cook 4 minutes, or until chicken is cooked through and no longer pink in the center; stir occasionally. Return vegetables to skillet. Add water. Season to taste with salt and pepper. Continue cooking for 2 minutes more, or until thoroughly heated. Warm tortillas in the microwave. Fill tortillas with chicken mixture.
Yield: 4 servings

Nutritional Facts per Serving:

510 Calories, 45 Fat Calories, 5g Fat, 1g Saturated Fat, 75mg Cholesterol, 1450mg Sodium, 78g Carbohydrate, 4g Dietary Fiber, 6g Sugars, 36g Protein, 30% (DV) Vitamin A, 110% (DV) Vitamin C, 2% (DV) Calcium, 25% (DV) Iron

Broiled Lemon Thyme Chicken

4 skinless, boneless chicken breast halves
$1/4$ cup Worcestershire sauce
2 tablespoons fresh lemon juice
1 teaspoon minced garlic
$1/2$ teaspoon freshly ground black pepper
$1/2$ teaspoon grated lemon peel
$1/4$ teaspoon minced fresh thyme (optional)

Lightly flatten chicken breasts to uniform thickness. In a small bowl, combine Worcestershire sauce, lemon juice, minced garlic, black pepper, and lemon peel; pour mixture over chicken breasts. Cover and allow to marinate 15 minutes, turning once. Remove chicken; reserve marinade. Place the chicken on a broiler pan that has been sprayed with nonstick cooking spray. Broil 4 to 5 inches from heat source for 3 to 4 minutes, then turn. Brush with marinade. Broil an additional 3 to 4 minutes, or until chicken is tender and no longer pink. Garnish with fresh thyme, if desired.
Yield: 4 servings

Nutritional Facts per Serving:
150 Calories, 30 Fat Calories, 3g Fat, 1g Saturated Fat, 70mg Cholesterol, 230mg Sodium, 4g Carbohydrate, 0g Dietary Fiber, 1g Sugars, 26g Protein, 0% (DV) Vitamin A, 10% (DV) Vitamin C, 4% (DV) Calcium, 10% (DV) Iron

Turkey and Cheese Burritos

1½ pounds ground turkey breast
1¼ cups prepared thick and chunky salsa
½ cup reduced-fat Monterey Jack cheese
8 fat-free flour tortillas, warmed
Thinly sliced lettuce
Chopped tomato
Sliced ripe olives

In large skillet, brown ground turkey over medium-high heat for 6 to 8 minutes, or until no longer pink. Pour off drippings. Stir in salsa and Monterey Jack cheese; heat until cheese melts and remove from flame. Spoon approximately ½ cup turkey mixture in the center of each tortilla. Fold bottom edge up over filling; fold sides to center, overlapping edges. Top with lettuce, tomato, and olives.
Yield: 4 servings

Nutritional Facts per Serving:

520 Calories, 50 Fat Calories, 6g Fat, 2g Saturated Fat, 125mg Cholesterol, 1680mg Sodium, 64g Carbohydrate, 4g Dietary Fiber, 7g Sugars, 53g Protein, 15% (DV) Vitamin A, 10% (DV) Vitamin C, 20% (DV) Calcium, 30% (DV) Iron

4

Beef

Easy Beef and Vegetable Stir-Fry

1 pound beef (top round or boneless top sirloin steak), cut 1 inch thick
$1/4$ cup plus 2 tablespoons water
2 tablespoons dry sherry
2 tablespoons reduced-sodium soy sauce
1 tablespoon cornstarch
2 teaspoons vegetable oil
1 garlic clove, crushed
1 (16-ounce) package frozen vegetable mix
2 cups cooked rice

Trim fat from meat. Cut steak lengthwise in half and then crosswise into $1/8$-inch strips and put aside. In a small bowl, combine $1/4$ cup water, sherry, soy sauce, and cornstarch; reserve. In a large nonstick skillet, heat oil over medium-high flame until hot. Add beef and garlic and stir-fry 1 to 2 minutes, or until outside surface is no longer pink. Remove from skillet with slotted spoon; keep warm. In same skillet, heat 2 tablespoons water until hot. Add vegetables; cook 5 minutes or until water has evaporated and vegetables are hot, stirring occasionally. Return beef to skillet and add sauce mixture; cook and stir until sauce is thickened and bubbly. Serve over rice.

Yield: 4 servings

Nutritional Facts per Serving:

360 Calories, 80 Fat Calories, 9g Fat, 3g Saturated Fat, 80mg Cholesterol, 770mg Sodium, 35g Carbohydrate, 6g Dietary Fiber, 4g Sugars, 33g Protein, 90% (DV) Vitamin A, 6% (DV) Vitamin C, 4% (DV) Calcium, 25% (DV) Iron

Broiled Soy-Marinated Flank Steak

$3/4$ cup green onion, thinly sliced
$1/2$ cup water
3 tablespoons fresh lemon juice
$2^1/2$ tablespoons reduced-sodium soy sauce
$1/2$ tablespoon olive oil
$3/4$ teaspoon dried oregano
$3/4$ teaspoon ground black pepper
$3/4$ pound lean flank steak
4 cups cooked rice

Combine onion, water, lemon juice, soy sauce, oil, oregano, and pepper. Spoon $1/4$ cup plus 2 tablespoons mixture into a measuring cup and set aside. Place remaining mixture into a zip-type plastic bag, along with flank steak. Seal and marinate in the refrigerator for 15 minutes. Remove steak from bag and discard marinade. Place steak on a broiling pan that has been sprayed with nonstick spray. Broil for approximately 8 minutes on each side, or to desired degree of doneness. Cut steak diagonally across the grain into very thin slices; set aside. Place reserved marinade into a small microwave-safe bowl and microwave on High for 40 seconds or until thoroughly heated. Serve with rice.
Yield: 6 servings

Nutritional Facts per Serving:

220 Calories, 50 Fat Calories, 6g Fat, 2g Saturated Fat, 30mg Cholesterol,

600mg Sodium, 26g Carbohydrate, 1g Dietary Fiber, 1g Sugars, 15g Protein, 2% (DV) Vitamin A, 10% (DV) Vitamin C, 2% (DV) Calcium, 10% (DV) Iron

Beefsteaks with Black Peppercorn Wine Sauce

4 eye of round steaks, 1 inch thick
1¹/₂ teaspoons cornstarch
1 cup reduced-sodium beef broth
¹/₈ teaspoon dried thyme, crushed
1 small bay leaf
2 tablespoons dry red wine
¹/₈ teaspoon black peppercorns, crushed
3 cups cooked rice

Heat large, heavy skillet over medium flame for 6 minutes. Place beef steaks in skillet and cook 10 to 14 minutes, turning once. Meanwhile, dissolve cornstarch in broth in a small saucepan. Bring to a boil and cook about 1 minute, or until slightly thickened. Stir in the thyme and bay leaf. Lower heat to medium and cook about 5 minutes or until reduced to ¹/₂ cup. Add wine and peppercorns; cook 4 minutes, stirring occasionally. Remove bay leaf. Spoon sauce over steaks.
Yield: 4 servings

Nutritional Facts per Serving:
420 Calories, 60 Fat Calories, 6g Fat, 2.5g Saturated Fat, 65mg Cholesterol, 390mg Sodium, 55g Carbohydrate, 5g Dietary Fiber, 3g Sugars, 34g Protein, 0% (DV) Vitamin A, 0% (DV) Vitamin C, 8% (DV) Calcium, 45% (DV) Iron

Beef-Pepper-and-Mushroom Kabobs

1 pound boneless top sirloin steak, 1 inch thick
1 tablespoon fresh lemon juice
1 tablespoon water
2 teaspoons Dijon mustard
1 teaspoon honey
1/2 teaspoon dried oregano, crushed
1/4 teaspoon freshly ground pepper
1 large green, red, or yellow pepper, cut into 1 1/4-inch pieces
12 large mushrooms
Salt
2 cups cooked rice

Trim fat from beef; cut into 1 1/4-inch pieces. In a large bowl, whisk together lemon juice, water, mustard, honey, oregano, and ground pepper; add beef, bell pepper, and mushrooms, tossing to coat. Alternately thread pieces of beef, bell pepper, and mushrooms on four metal skewers. Place kabobs on broiler pan and broil 3 to 4 inches from heat. Broil 9 to 12 minutes for medium-rare to medium doneness, turning occasionally. Season to taste with salt. Serve with rice.

Yield: 4 servings

Nutritional Facts per Serving:

330 Calories, 60 Fat Calories, 7g Fat, 2.5g Saturated Fat, 75mg Cholesterol, 650mg Sodium, 35g Carbohydrate, 2g Dietary Fiber, 3g Sugars, 30g Protein, 15% (DV) Vitamin A, 60% (DV) Vitamin C, 4% (DV) Calcium, 30% (DV) Iron

Seafood

Crispy Baked Fish

4 sea bass fillets
³/₄ cup bread crumbs
1 teaspoon Parmesan cheese
1 tablespoon fresh tarragon (or ¹/₂ teaspoon dried)
¹/₂ teaspoon paprika
Salt and freshly ground pepper
1 lemon, cut into wedges (optional)

Rinse fillets in cold water. In a small bowl combine the bread crumbs, Parmesan cheese, tarragon, paprika, salt, and pepper. Dredge fillets in the bread crumb mixture; coat both sides. Spray a large baking dish with nonstick spray and arrange fillets in the baking dish. Bake uncovered at 450 degrees F for approximately 8 to 12 minutes, depending on the thickness of the fillets. Do not turn during baking. Serve with lemon wedges, if desired.

Yield: 4 servings

Nutritional Facts per Serving:

170 Calories, 30 Fat Calories, 3g Fat, .5g Saturated Fat, 75mg Cholesterol, 480mg Sodium, 13g Carbohydrate, <1g Dietary Fiber, 1g Sugars, 20g Protein, 4% (DV) Vitamin A, 0% (DV) Vitamin C, 6% (DV) Calcium, 10% (DV) Iron

Honey-Mustard Tuna

1 tablespoon Dijon mustard
1 tablespoon sugar
2 tablespoons honey
3 tablespoons soy sauce
4 tuna steaks

In a small bowl, mix the mustard, sugar, honey, and soy sauce together to blend. Preheat the broiler or grill. Place the tuna steaks on a broiling pan coated with nonstick spray. Broil the tuna for approximately 5 minutes. Remove from oven and brush the honey-mustard glaze on each steak. Return to the broiler and cook for 4 to 5 more minutes, or until the tuna feels firm to the touch and is cooked throughout. Remove the fish from broiling pan and arrange on plates. Brush each steak with the honey-mustard glaze again and serve.
Yield: 4 servings

Nutritional Facts per Serving:
210 Calories, 15 Fat Calories, 1.5g Fat, 0g Saturated Fat, 65mg Cholesterol, 920mg Sodium, 13g Carbohydrate, 0g Dietary Fiber, 11g Sugars, 35g Protein, 2% (DV) Vitamin A, 2% (DV) Vitamin C, 4% (DV) Calcium, 8% (DV) Iron

Perfect Peppered Tuna Steak

4 tuna steaks
$1/2$ tablespoon olive oil
Cracked black pepper
1 lemon, cut into wedges (optional)

Brush both sides of the tuna steak with the oil. Place the tuna on a broiler pan and sprinkle the cracked pepper on the tops of the steaks. Broil the tuna steaks for approximately 5 minutes. Turn the steaks over and sprinkle with more cracked pepper and broil for an additional 5 minutes, or until the fish is cooked thoroughly. Arrange on plates and garnish with lemon wedges, if desired.
Yield: 4 servings

Nutritional Facts per Serving:
180 Calories, 25 Fat Calories, 3g Fat, .5g Saturated Fat, 65mg Cholesterol, 55mg Sodium, 2g Carbohydrate, 0g Dietary Fiber, 0g Sugars, 34g Protein, 2% (DV) Vitamin A, 15% (DV) Vitamin C, 4% (DV) Calcium, 8% (DV) Iron

Garlic Chili Shrimp over Capellini

3 teaspoons chili sauce
2 teaspoons soy sauce
1 teaspoon fat-free chicken broth
2 teaspoons honey
1/2 teaspoon ginger powder
1/8 teaspoon crushed red pepper flakes (optional)
4 green onions, minced
2 garlic cloves, minced
1 teaspoon canola oil
1 1/4 pounds shrimp, peeled and deveined
8 ounces cooked capellini (angel hair) pasta

Combine the chili sauce, soy sauce, broth, honey, ginger, and red pepper flakes, if using. Cook the onions and garlic in the oil in a nonstick skillet over medium-high heat just until the onions are tender, about 4 minutes. Transfer to a medium bowl. Add shrimp to skillet. Cook for 2 minutes. Pour in the sauce mixture and cook until shrimp turn opaque, 4 to 5 minutes, stirring frequently. Toss with onion-garlic mixture and serve over hot capellini.

Yield: 4 servings

Nutritional Facts per Serving:

290 Calories, 50 Fat Calories, 6g Fat, .5g Saturated Fat, 200mg Cholesterol, 470mg Sodium, 30g Carbohydrate, 5g Dietary Fiber, 6g Sugars, 27g Protein, 100% (DV) Vitamin A, 15% (DV) Vitamin C, 8% (DV) Calcium, 30% (DV) Iron

Grilled Swordfish with Roasted Peppers

$3/4$ cup fat-free plain yogurt
$3/4$ cup fat-free mayonnaise
1 shallot, minced
1 tablespoon minced fresh tarragon (or 1 teaspoon dried)
$1/2$ tablespoon freshly ground pepper
Juice of 1 lemon
3 tablespoons skim milk
4 swordfish (or tuna) steaks
2 roasted red peppers, cut into strips
1 lemon, cut into wedges (optional)

In a baking dish combine the yogurt, mayonnaise, shallot, tarragon, ground pepper, lemon juice, and milk. Dredge swordfish in the mixture; coat both sides. Marinate 15 minutes, turning once. Spray grill with nonstick cooking spray. Grill swordfish for approximately 5 minutes; baste; and turn the fish to cook on the other side for approximately 5 minutes more, or until lightly golden on the outside and cooked through. Transfer to a serving plate and add the roasted red pepper strips. Garnish with fresh lemon wedges, if desired.
Yield: 4 servings

Nutritional Facts per Serving:
230 Calories, 50 Fat Calories, 6g Fat, 1.5g Saturated Fat, 55mg Cholesterol, 520mg Sodium, 12g Carbohydrate, <1g Dietary Fiber, 7g Sugars, 30g Protein, 25% (DV) Vitamin A, 30% (DV) Vitamin C, 10% (DV) Calcium, 8% (DV) Iron

Super Herbed Scampi with Linguine

2 teaspoons extra-virgin olive oil
3 garlic cloves, minced
1 teaspoon grated lemon peel
³/₄ teaspoon dried thyme
³/₄ teaspoon dried oregano
¹/₄ teaspoon freshly ground pepper
³/₄ pound medium shrimp, peeled and deveined
3 (8-ounce) cans low-sodium tomato sauce
¹/₄ cup minced parsley
8 ounces linguine, cooked and drained
2 teaspoons grated Parmesan cheese

In a bowl mix the oil, garlic, lemon peel, thyme, oregano, and black pepper together. Add the shrimp and toss to coat. In a nonstick skillet over medium-high heat sauté the shrimp mixture for 2 minutes, stirring often. Add tomato sauce. Bring to a boil. Reduce heat to medium and simmer, stirring often until shrimp turns pink, 4 to 5 minutes. Stir in parsley. Pour sauce over hot linguine and sprinkle with Parmesan cheese. Serve at once.
Yield: 4 servings

Nutritional Facts per Serving:

280 Calories, 60 Fat Calories, 7g Fat, 1.5g Saturated Fat, 140mg Cholesterol, 430mg Sodium, 31g Carbohydrate, 4g Dietary Fiber, 7g Sugars, 24g Protein, 45% (DV) Vitamin A, 50% (DV) Vitamin C, 10% (DV) Calcium, 30% (DV) Iron

Garlic Skewered Shrimp

1 pound large shrimp, peeled and deveined
2 tablespoons reduced-sodium soy sauce
1/2 tablespoon vegetable oil
3 garlic cloves, minced
1/4 teaspoon crushed red pepper flakes (optional)
2 green onions, minced
1 green bell pepper, cut into 1-inch squares
8 cherry tomatoes

Place shrimp in a large plastic zip-type bag. Combine soy sauce, oil, garlic, red pepper, and onion in a small bowl; mix well. Pour over shrimp. Close bag; shake to coat. Marinate for 10 minutes. Drain shrimp; reserve marinade. Alternately thread shrimp, bell pepper, and cherry tomatoes on skewers. Brush with reserved marinade; discard remainder. Place on rack of broiling pan or grill. Broil or grill for 5 minutes; turn shrimp and broil or grill an additional 5 minutes, or until shrimp are opaque. Serve with rice.
Yield: 4 servings

Nutritional Facts per Serving:
120 Calories, 25 Fat Calories, 3g Fat, .5g Saturated Fat, 160mg Cholesterol, 850mg Sodium, 5g Carbohydrate, <1g Dietary Fiber, 2g Sugars, 18g Protein, 10% (DV) Vitamin A, 40% (DV) Vitamin C, 4% (DV) Calcium, 15% (DV) Iron

Grilled Citrus Fish

$^1/_2$ cup bottled chili sauce
3 tablespoons frozen orange juice concentrate
2 tablespoons fresh lemon juice
1 tablespoon Worcestershire sauce
1 tablespoon olive oil
4 fresh cod fillets
Chopped fresh parsley
1 lemon, cut into wedges (optional)

In a small bowl, combine chili sauce, orange juice concentrate, lemon juice, Worcestershire sauce, and oil. Place fish in a baking dish. Pour marinade over fillets, turning to coat. Cover and refrigerate for 15 minutes. Coat grill with nonstick cooking spray and preheat. Place fish fillets on grill. Cook approximately 6 minutes on each side, allowing at least 10 minutes per inch of thickness. Fish is done when it flakes easily and is no longer opaque. Sprinkle with fresh parsley. Garnish with lemon wedges, if desired.
Yield: 4 servings

Nutritional Facts per Serving:
260 Calories, 45 Fat Calories, 5g Fat, 1g Saturated Fat, 100mg Cholesterol, 630mg Sodium, 11g Carbohydrate, <1g Dietary Fiber, 6g Sugars, 42g Protein, 10% (DV) Vitamin A, 30% (DV) Vitamin C, 4% (DV) Calcium, 8% (DV) Iron

New Mexican Snapper

4 red snapper fillets
Salt and freshly ground pepper
$^1/_2$ cup salsa
1 tomato, chopped
$^1/_4$ cup green onions, sliced
$^1/_4$ cup fresh cilantro, chopped
1 lime, cut into wedges (optional)

Place fish in a shallow baking dish. Season to taste with salt and pepper. Cover; bake at 400 degrees F until fish flakes easily, about 10 minutes per inch of thickness. Pour off juices. Spoon the salsa evenly over fish. Top with tomato and onions. Bake uncovered until heated throughout, about 5 minutes. Sprinkle with cilantro. Garnish with lime wedges, if desired.

Yield: 4 servings

Nutritional Facts per Serving:

200 Calories, 25 Fat Calories, 2.5g Fat, .5g Saturated Fat, 65mg Cholesterol, 770mg Sodium, 4g Carbohydrate, <1g Dietary Fiber, 2g Sugars, 38g Protein, 10% (DV) Vitamin A, 15% (DV) Vitamin C, 10% (DV) Calcium, 4% (DV) Iron

Scallop Stir-Fry

6 ounces uncooked ramen noodles
1 teaspoon vegetable oil
1 pound asparagus, cut into 1-inch pieces
1 red bell pepper, cut into thin strips
3 green onions, chopped
1 garlic clove, minced
3/4 pound sea scallops, halved
2 tablespoon reduced-sodium soy sauce
1 teaspoon hot pepper sauce
1 teaspoon sesame oil
Juice of 1/2 lemon

Cook noodles in boiling water according to package directions. Drain
and set aside. In a large wok or skillet, heat oil over high flame and
add asparagus, bell pepper, onions, and garlic. Stir-fry for 2 minutes.
Add scallops; stir-fry until scallops are opaque. Stir in soy sauce, hot
sauce, sesame oil, and lemon juice. Add cooked noodles; heat thoroughly, stirring occasionally.
Yield: 4 servings

Nutritional Facts per Serving:
210 Calories, 60 Fat Calories, 6g Fat, 1g Saturated Fat, 35mg Cholesterol, 1750mg Sodium, 25g Carbohydrate, 5g Dietary Fiber, 5g Sugars,
16g Protein, 60% (DV) Vitamin A, 110% (DV) Vitamin C, 6% (DV) Calcium, 15% (DV) Iron

Pasta

Farfalle with Fresh Tomatoes and Basil

1 pound farfalle (bow tie) pasta
1 1/2 pounds (4 cups) ripe tomatoes, cored and cut into 1/2-inch diced
  pieces
2 tablespoons extra-virgin olive oil
1/4 cup coarsely chopped fresh basil leaves
1 small garlic clove crushed through press
1/2 teaspoon salt
Grated Parmigiano-Reggiano cheese (optional)

In a large pot of boiling water, cook pasta, stirring occasionally to prevent clumping, until al dente (firm to the bite), approximately 10 to 12 minutes. Meanwhile, in a large serving bowl, combine tomatoes, oil, basil, garlic, and salt; set aside. Drain cooked pasta in colander; shake well. Add immediately to tomato mixture. Toss gently to combine. Top with cheese, if desired, and serve.
Yield: 6 servings

Nutritional Facts per Serving:

320 Calories, 60 Fat Calories, 6g Fat, 1g Saturated Fat, 0mg Cholesterol, 200mg Sodium, 55g Carbohydrate, 3g Dietary Fiber, 5g Sugars, 10g Protein, 15% (DV) Vitamin A, 35% (DV) Vitamin C, 4% (DV) Calcium, 15% (DV) Iron

Low-Fat Fettuccine Alfredo

1 pound fettuccine
2 teaspoons olive oil
$^1/_2$ cup fat-free sour cream
1 (12-ounce) can evaporated skim milk
5 tablespoons freshly grated Parmesan cheese
2 tablespoons minced fresh Italian parsley
1 tablespoon fresh basil, minced
Pinch of red pepper flakes, crushed
Salt and freshly ground pepper
2 garlic cloves, minced

Cook pasta according to package directions. Drain. Place the pasta back in the pot and toss with oil. Add sour cream, milk, Parmesan, parsley, basil, red pepper, salt and pepper to taste, and garlic. Cook over low heat until thick and bubbling, stirring constantly. Serve immediately.
Yield: 6 servings

Nutritional Facts per Serving:

400 Calories, 40 Fat Calories, 4.5g Fat, 1.5g Saturated Fat, 5mg Cholesterol, 410mg Sodium, 70g Carbohydrate, 3g Dietary Fiber, 11g Sugars, 18g Protein, 10% (DV) Vitamin A, 4% (DV) Vitamin C, 30% (DV) Calcium, 20% (DV) Iron

Fusilli Primavera

12 ounces broccoli, chopped
1 yellow bell pepper, thinly sliced
1 tablespoon extra-virgin olive oil
3 garlic cloves, minced
$^1/_2$ cup fat-free chicken broth
$1^1/_2$ teaspoons Dijon mustard
8 ounces fusilli pasta, cooked and drained
8 ripe cherry tomatoes, halved
4 teaspoons white wine vinegar
2 tablespoons fresh parsley, minced
Freshly grated Parmesan cheese (optional)

In a nonstick skillet over medium heat, cook broccoli and bell pepper in the oil for 3 minutes, or until crisp-tender. Add garlic and cook for an additional 2 minutes. In a small bowl mix broth and mustard. Stir into broccoli mixture and bring to a boil. In a large bowl, toss the broccoli mixture with the pasta. Add tomatoes, drizzle with vinegar, and toss again. Sprinkle with fresh chopped parsley. Top with freshly grated Parmesan cheese, if desired.
Yield: 4 servings

Nutritional Facts per Serving:
260 Calories, 45 Fat Calories, 5g Fat, .5g Saturated Fat, 0mg Cholesterol, 470mg Sodium, 45g Carbohydrate, 5g Dietary Fiber, 5g Sugars, 10g Protein, 30% (DV) Vitamin A, 180% (DV) Vitamin C, 6% (DV) Calcium, 20% (DV) Iron

Pomodoro Veggie Pasta Bake

3 cups cooked ziti pasta
1 (27¹/₂-ounce) jar fat-free pasta sauce
1¹/₂ cups fat-free mozzarella, shredded
2 cups sliced mushrooms
2 cups zucchini, thinly sliced
2 cups yellow squash, thinly sliced
¹/₂ cup fat-free grated cheese

Mix pasta, sauce, 1 cup of the mozzarella cheese, mushrooms, zucchini, squash, and ¹/₄ cup of the grated topping. Place into a 13 × 9-inch baking dish. Top with remaining mozzarella cheese and remaining ¹/₄ cup grated topping. Bake at 350 degrees F for 15 to 20 minutes, or until heated throughout.
Yield: 8 servings

Nutritional Facts per Serving:
180 Calories, 5 Fat Calories, .5g Fat, 0g Saturated Fat, 0mg Cholesterol, 850mg Sodium, 30g Carbohydrate, 4g Dietary Fiber, 9g Sugars, 16g Protein, 35% (DV) Vitamin A, 40% (DV) Vitamin C, 50% (DV) Calcium, 15% (DV) Iron

Springtime Asparagus Rotini Pasta

2 tablespoons reduced-fat margarine
$1/4$ cup onion, finely chopped
3 garlic cloves, minced
8 ounces fresh asparagus, sliced diagonally into 1-inch pieces
2 tablespoons dry white wine
2 tablespoons fresh lemon juice
Freshly ground pepper
8 ounces rotini pasta, cooked and drained
$1/4$ cup fat-free grated cheese topping
1 cup fat-free mozzarella, shredded

Melt margarine over medium heat in a large nonstick skillet. Add onion and garlic and cook, stirring, until soft. Do not brown. Add asparagus and continue to cook for an additional 2 minutes. Add wine and lemon juice. Season to taste with pepper. Remove from heat. In a large bowl, toss hot pasta, cheese, and the asparagus mixture. Remove to serving platter. Top with the mozzarella. Serve immediately.
Yield: 4 servings

Nutritional Facts per Serving:
310 Calories, 50 Fat Calories, 6g Fat, 1.5g Saturated Fat, 5mg Cholesterol, 420mg Sodium, 43g Carbohydrate, 3g Dietary Fiber, 5g Sugars, 19g Protein, 20% (DV) Vitamin A, 15% (DV) Vitamin C, 50% (DV) Calcium, 15% (DV) Iron

Pasta Fresca

1 tablespoon extra-virgin olive oil

1 medium zucchini, sliced

2 tablespoons chopped shallots

2 large garlic cloves, minced

1 large tomato, diced

2 tablespoons fresh basil, minced

2 tablespoons fat-free grated cheese topping

12 ounces ziti, cooked and drained

Heat oil in a large nonstick skillet. Place zucchini in skillet and cook for 1 minute. Add shallots and garlic; stir over heat for 2 minutes. Stir in tomato. Add basil and cheese; cook for 30 seconds. Remove from heat. Pour over hot ziti and serve at once.

Yield: 4 servings

Nutritional Facts per Serving:

320 Calories, 40 Fat Calories, 4.5g Fat, 1g Saturated Fat, 0mg Cholesterol, 65mg Sodium, 58g Carbohydrate, 3g Dietary Fiber, 4g Sugars, 11g Protein, 6% (DV) Vitamin A, 10% (DV) Vitamin C, 6% (DV) Calcium, 15% (DV) Iron

Shells and Cheddar Bake

1¹/₂ cups skim milk
2 teaspoons cornstarch
¹/₂ teaspoon dry mustard
¹/₄ teaspoon freshly ground black pepper
¹/₄ teaspoon hot pepper sauce
1 cup shredded fat-free Cheddar
³/₄ cup fat-free cottage cheese
8 ounces small shell pasta, cooked and drained
1 package frozen chopped spinach, thawed and squeezed dry
    (optional)
¹/₄ cup green onion, minced
1 teaspoon Italian flavored bread crumbs

Coat a 9-inch square baking dish with nonstick cooking spray. In a
medium saucepan, whisk milk, cornstarch, mustard, pepper, and hot
sauce until smooth. Cook over medium-high heat, stirring constantly,
until sauce thickens and comes to a low boil. Add the Cheddar and the
cottage cheese. Cook until the cheese is melted and well blended. In a
large bowl, combine the cheese sauce, pasta, spinach, if using, and
onions. Pour into baking dish. Top with bread crumbs. Bake at 400 degrees F until hot and bubbly, about 15 minutes.
Yield: 4 servings

Nutritional Facts per Serving:

360 Calories, 15 Fat Calories, 1.5g Fat, 0g Saturated Fat, 5mg Cholesterol, 470mg Sodium, 59g Carbohydrate, 4g Dietary Fiber, 8g Sugars,
27g Protein, 130% (DV) Vitamin A, 20% (DV) Vitamin C, 70% (DV) Calcium, 20% (DV) Iron

7

Fun Food for Kids

Why not try getting the kids involved in helping to prepare some fun and easy foods and
snacks? It's a good way to get them interested
in healthy eating.

Fun Snacks

- Use cookie cutters to cut sandwiches into fun
  shapes.

- Top waffles or pancakes with fresh fruit and
  roll them up.

- Create an edible "mouse" using a canned
  pear half for the body, cheese for the tail,
  raisins for eyes, and almond slivers for ears.

- Vegetable soup is a clever way to get kids to
  eat their vegetables. Make it kid-friendly by

adding alphabet pasta or fun animal-shaped pasta.

- Prepare a fat-free dip to serve with assorted raw veggies.

- Choose sherbet, angel food cake, frozen fruit bars, or low-fat frozen yogurt instead of high-fat desserts.

- Funny Face Pizzas can be made easily: Using a pita bread for the base, cover with fat-free pasta sauce and fat-free mozzarella cheese, add 2 zucchini rounds for eyes, a triangle piece of bell pepper for the nose, and a slice of tomato or mushroom for the mouth. Experiment with your child's favorite veggies.

- Salad Kabobs are quick and easy: Cut your child's favorite cheese and veggies into cubes and alternate on a skewer. Serve with a fat-free dip.

- Sweet and Fruity Kabobs are great fun cooked indoors or out: Preheat a broiler or grill. Using bananas, melon, kiwi, pineapple, and marshmallows, cut fruit into chunks; alternate pieces of fruit and marshmallow on a skewer. In a small bowl combine 1 tablespoon honey with 1 tablespoon lemon juice, mix well. Brush each kabob with the honey-lemon mixture and broil or grill, turning just until marshmallow begins to turn light golden. Allow to cool before serving.

Desserts

Fresh Seasonal Fruit with Vanilla Sauce

3 ounces fat-free cream cheese
1/2 cup brown sugar, packed
1/2 teaspoon vanilla
1 cup fat-free plain yogurt
8 cups assorted fresh fruit (bananas, strawberries, pineapple, honey-
    dew), cut up

In a small mixing bowl combine the cream cheese, brown sugar, and vanilla. Beat with an electric mixer until fluffy. Add yogurt; beat until smooth. Serve over fresh fruit.
Yield: 8 servings

Nutritional Facts per Serving:

160 Calories, 5 Fat Calories, .5g Fat, 0g Saturated Fat, 0mg Cholesterol, 85mg Sodium, 37g Carbohydrate, 2g Dietary Fiber, 33g Sugars, 4g Protein, 4% (DV) Vitamin A, 70% (DV) Vitamin C, 10% (DV) Calcium, 4% (DV) Iron

Angel Food Cake with Raspberry Sauce

10 ounces fresh raspberries, plus raspberries for garnish
2 teaspoons fresh lemon juice
$1/3$ cup confectioners' sugar
1 prepared angel food cake
Mint sprigs (optional)

Place raspberries in a blender. Pour in the lemon juice and sugar. Purée. Pass through a strainer, discarding solids. Place a slice of angel food cake on each plate, top with the raspberry sauce, and garnish with fresh mint and additional raspberries.

Yield: 8 servings

Nutritional Facts per Serving:

130 Calories, 5 Fat Calories, .5g Fat, 0g Saturated Fat, 0mg Cholesterol, 280mg Sodium, 31g Carbohydrate, 2g Dietary Fiber, 26g Sugars, 3g Protein, 0% (DV) Vitamin A, 15% (DV) Vitamin C, 6% (DV) Calcium, 2% (DV) Iron

Fresh Strawberries with Balsamic Vinegar over Vanilla Ice Cream

2 tablespoons balsamic vinegar
4 tablespoons sugar
2 (1-pint) baskets of fresh strawberries, washed, hulled, and sliced
4 cups fat-free vanilla ice cream
Mint sprigs (optional)

In a small bowl, combine the balsamic vinegar and sugar. Stir until sugar has dissolved and blended with the vinegar. Place strawberries in a medium bowl and pour the vinegar mixture over the berries. Toss gently. Scoop vanilla ice cream into serving bowls and top with strawberries. Garnish with fresh mint, if desired.
Yield: 4 servings

Nutritional Facts per Serving:
240 Calories, 0 Fat Calories, 0g Fat, 0g Saturated Fat, 0mg Cholesterol, 110mg Sodium, 58g Carbohydrate, 3g Dietary Fiber, 56g Sugars, 6g Protein, 10% (DV) Vitamin A, 160% (DV) Vitamin C, 20% (DV) Calcium, 4% (DV) Iron

Fresh Fruit with
Fat-Free Chocolate Dip

1 pear, cut into wedges
1 apple, thinly sliced
1/2 cup water plus the juice of 1/2 lemon
8 ounces fat-free chocolate dip
1/4 pound green grapes
1/4 pound red grapes
2 kiwis, peeled and thinly sliced
1 star fruit, thinly sliced
1/2 pint strawberries
Mint sprigs (optional)

After slicing pear and apple, immerse in lemon-water mixture to prevent oxidation. Remove fruit slices and pat dry. Place small bowl with chocolate dip in the center of a serving platter. Surround with the fruit. Garnish with fresh mint, if desired.

Yield: 4 servings

Nutritional Facts per Serving:
150 Calories, 0 Fat Calories, 0g Fat, 0g Saturated Fat, 0mg Cholesterol, 65mg Sodium, 38g Carbohydrate, 4g Dietary Fiber, 32g Sugars, 3g Protein, 8% (DV) Vitamin A, 90% (DV) Vitamin C, 8% (DV) Calcium, 4% (DV) Iron

Berries with Honey-Yogurt Sauce

1 cup fat-free plain yogurt
1 tablespoon orange juice
2 teaspoons honey
$1/2$ teaspoon ground cinnamon
3 cups fresh strawberries, rinsed and hulled
1 cup blueberries, rinsed
Mint sprigs (optional)

Combine yogurt, orange juice, honey, and cinnamon in a small bowl until well blended. Divide strawberries and blueberries into 4 serving dishes. Spoon sauce over the berries. Garnish with fresh mint, if desired.
Yield: 4 servings

Nutritional Facts per Serving:

100 Calories, 5 Fat Calories, .5g Fat, 0g Saturated Fat, 0mg Cholesterol, 50mg Sodium, 21g Carbohydrate, 3g Dietary Fiber, 18g Sugars, 4g Protein, 2% (DV) Vitamin A, 110% (DV) Vitamin C, 15% Calcium, 4% (DV) Iron

Index

*Divide and conquer your surroundings
on your way to a more organized and
less chaotic life with the help of . . .*

ROBYN FREEDMAN SPIZMAN

KITCHEN 101

Setting up a kitchen can be a daunting job for new homeowners and cooking novices. But even so-called veterans can be clueless when it comes to stocking a pantry or determining food freshness. KITCHEN 101 offers helpful advice from setup to cleanup.

QUICK TIPS FOR BUSY PEOPLE

Always on the run? Do you find yourself in a race against time? QUICK TIPS FOR BUSY PEOPLE is the perfect solution for anyone who is on the go and wants to save time, money, and energy.

Published by Ivy Books.
Available wherever books are sold.